KUNG FU

Pamela Randall

The Rosen Publishing Group's
PowerKids Press™
New York

Published in 1999 by The Rosen Publishing Group, Inc.
29 East 21st Street, New York, NY 10010

First Edition

Book Design: Danielle Primiceri

Photo Illustrations by Seth Dinnerman

Randall, Pamela.
   Kung fu / by Pamela Randall.
      p. cm.—(Martial arts)
   Includes index.
   Summary: Introduces the history, basic moves, and terminology of this martial art.
   ISBN 0-8239-5237-1
   1. Kung fu—Juvenile literature. [1. Kung fu.]   I. Title.
II. Series: Randall, Pamela. Martial arts.
GV1114.7.R36 1998
796.815'9—dc21   97-49272
                                              CIP
                                              AC

Manufactured in the United States of America

Contents

Pete and Erin, the Movie Fans

Pete and his friend Erin love to watch movies. Some of their favorites are **martial arts** (MAR-shul ARTS) movies. Erin likes to watch the heroes defeat the bad guys. Pete isn't small for his age, but at nine, he's still not very big yet. When he looks at the powerful heroes in martial arts movies, he wishes he could be like them.

Erin and Pete each asked their parents if they would let them study martial arts. Soon, they were both signed up for kung fu school.

◄ *Signing up for martial arts lessons with a friend can be fun.*

Kung Fu: An Ancient Art

Kung fu was created in China almost 5,000 years ago. Today there are many different styles of this martial art. Some forms of kung fu are very **aggressive** (uh-GREH-siv). Other forms are more **defensive** (dih-FEN-siv). Some forms of kung fu even include **acrobatic** (a-kroh-BA-tik) exercises.

As students of kung fu practice in their classes, they also learn about Chinese **culture** (KUL-cher) and history.

Some forms of kung fu include the use of weapons. But they are only used for show. People who practice kung fu don't use weapons to hurt each other. ▶

Monks and Warriors

Many centuries ago, several different kinds of people practiced kung fu—just like today. The first great emperor of China had his armies learn kung fu so they could use it when fighting. **Taoist** (DOW-ist) monks also learned kung fu to protect themselves and their land from robbers.

Kung fu is still practiced in China and all over the world. The styles of kung fu may vary from place to place. For example, the style practiced in southern China has many hand moves. In northern China, people practicing kung fu use their legs more than their hands.

Different styles of kung fu can be found in different parts of China.

9

The Words

The word *kung* means **"discipline"** (DIH-sih-plin) in Chinese. *Fu* means "person." Kung fu, then, means a disciplined person. But kung fu is about more than just fighting or discipline. Kung fu teaches that it's important to develop yourself in three areas.

The first of those areas is character, known in kung fu as ***dar*** (DAR). The second is mental ability, known as ***tse*** (tuh-SAY). The third area is physical ability, called ***tee*** (TEE).

Kung fu instructors teach their students how discipline can help them do better as they practice kung fu. ▶

Different Styles

One popular style, or school, of kung fu is *shaolin*. *Shaolin* began around 525 AD when a **Buddhist** (BOO-dist) monk from India named *Bodhidharma*, or *Tamo* in Chinese, traveled to China. He joined a temple of Buddhist monks and saw that they had trouble performing basic **meditation** (meh-dih-TAY-shun). Tamo taught them exercises based on the movements of animals, such as tigers. The exercises helped the monks to meditate and to defend themselves against local bandits. A form of these moves soon became known as *Shaolin Ssu,* or young forest temple, kung fu.

◀ *Meditation calms the mind and relaxes the body before and after practicing kung fu.*

Learning Kung Fu

A kung fu school is called a *kwoon* (KWOON). This is true whether classes are held in a special building, in someone's home, or outdoors in a field.

Kung fu teachers are called *sifu* (SEE-foo). Students learn to respect their teacher and the other students in their class. They are taught to behave that way outside of school too. Students who study for a long time and behave well are allowed to help teach new students.

It's a good idea to watch your kung fu teacher carefully.
This will help you learn new moves. ▶

Many Forms

Most kinds of kung fu use lots of punching and kicking. Others involve **grappling** (GRAP-ling) with and throwing an **opponent** (uh-POH-nent). Most forms teach fighting both with and without weapons. But there isn't one single way that's the right way.

There are many styles of kung fu and all these styles are more than just sports or styles of fighting. Kung fu is considered a way of life. This is because nearly all kinds of kung fu teach breathing, meditation, and discipline. All of these things can help students feel better about themselves in everything they do.

◀ *Learning kung fu moves can be a lot of fun, but there's more to kung fu than moves.*

An Ancient Technique

A common move in kung fu is called **diagonal striking** (dy-A-guh-nul STRY-king). This move comes from the oldest Chinese martial art, *shuaichiao*.

In this move, Pete's friend Kara steps out with her left foot. With her left hand across her body, she is able to block an opponent.

Kara can then grab
her opponent with
her left hand.
She will pull
him toward
one side of her
body. At the
same time, Kara
will strike him
with her right palm.

19

Black Belts, Bright Belts, No Belts

American and European students often feel that it's important to be **promoted** (pruh-MOH-ted) in their martial art. Students there often wear belts around their waists that show what rank, or skill level, each student has reached. The belts are sometimes called sashes.

Each level has its own color belt. The colors are usually bright—except for black belts. Only the highest-ranking students wear black belts. In China, students don't wear sashes. Rank is not very important there.

◄ *Unlike most martial arts, kung fu students wear black uniforms instead of white.*

Erin and Pete Learn a Lot

Pete and Erin have been taking kung fu lessons for almost six months. They've learned to punch, kick, and avoid their opponents' hands and feet. They have also learned to sit quietly and meditate.

Erin and Pete now understand what the actors are doing in kung fu movies. They know the names of some of the moves they see on the screen. Pete and Erin probably won't star in a kung fu movie. But now that they practice kung fu they enjoy the movies even more.

Glossary

acrobatic (a-kroh-BA-tik) Something that requires gymnastic skills.

aggressive (uh-GREH-siv) When someone starts a fight.

Buddhist (BOO-dist) A person who practices the religion of Buddhism.

culture (KUL-cher) The beliefs, customs, art, and religions of a group of people.

dar (DAR) A word used in kung fu that means character.

defensive (dih-FEN-siv) When someone guards against an attack.

diagonal striking (dy-A-guh-nul STRY-king) A way of hitting an opponent with your hand using a slanting motion.

discipline (DIH-sih-plin) Training the mind or character.

grappling (GRAP–ling) A kind of fighting that is a bit like wrestling.

kwoon (KWOON) A kung fu school.

martial art (MAR-shul ART) Any of the arts of self-defense or fighting that is practiced as sport.

meditation (meh-dih-TAY-shun) When you sit quietly and empty your mind of thoughts.

opponent (uh-POH-nent) A person who is on the other side in a fight.

promoted (pruh-MOH-ted) To be raised in rank or importance.

sifu (SEE-foo) A kung fu teacher.

Taoist (DOW-ist) Related to a Chinese religion that stresses harmony.

tee (TEE) A word used in kung fu that means physical ability.

tse (tuh-SAY) A word used in kung fu that means mental ability.

23

Index